THE **SMART** START RN

THE **SMART** START RN

Money Decisions That Compound for Decades

Steve R. Reckons, RN, MPA, BS Finance

The RN Wealth Series

An imprint of GAMS Relevance, LLC

Copyright

Copyright © 2026 GAMS Relevance, LLC
All rights reserved.

Disclaimer

This book is provided for informational and educational purposes only. It does not constitute financial, legal, medical, or professional advice. The author makes no representations or warranties regarding the accuracy or completeness of the information contained herein and shall not be liable for any losses or damages arising from its use.

Editorial Process Note

This series is organized around career phases, not personal failure. Nursing careers do not progress in straight lines. Capacity changes over time. Decisions that once felt manageable can later feel costly—not because they were wrong, but because conditions evolved.

This work was developed through a combination of original conceptual frameworks and professional analysis. Limited use of editing tools, including artificial intelligence–assisted drafting support, may have been used to improve clarity and support revisions. All concepts, structure, and final editorial decisions represent the author's intent and judgment.

ISBN: 978-1-972505-00-7

Published by
GAMS Relevance Press
An imprint of GAMS Relevance, LLC
Oklahoma City, Oklahoma
Printed in the United States of America

First Edition

For bulk orders, speaking inquiries, or institutional partnerships:
hello@gamsrelevance.com

Editor's Page

This book benefited from the careful editorial review of Keyonda Dean, **APRN, PMHNP.**

Her contributions focused on clarity, structure, and coherence—ensuring that the ideas presented here remain accessible without losing precision or restraint. Particular attention was given to maintaining consistency of tone across chapters and preserving the book's emphasis on context rather than prescription.

The author is grateful for her professionalism, insight, and attention to detail.

Author's Note

This series was written slowly and deliberately—not because the ideas are complex, but because the stakes are real.

Nurses are often given financial advice that assumes unlimited energy, stable schedules, and a career that progresses in a straight line. Real nursing careers do not unfold that way. Capacity changes. Priorities shift. What once felt manageable can later feel costly.

These books attempt to name those realities without drama. They do not promise transformation, optimization, or escape. They do not offer shortcuts or guarantees. Instead, they focus on structure—how early decisions compound, how income behaves at mid-career, and how stability becomes more important as capacity changes.

The goal of this series is not to motivate action. It is to reduce pressure.

If something here feels familiar rather than exciting, that is intentional. These books are designed for repeated reference—providing language for patterns you may already recognize, and clarity before decisions are forced.

Engage with what is relevant to your situation and disregard what does not apply. There is no urgency built into this work.

Preface

Why This Book Exists

Most financial books assume one reader: one level of energy, one moment in a career, one definition of success.

Nursing does not work that way.

Early in a nursing career, decisions feel small. Debt, lifestyle, and income choices are often framed as temporary or easily reversible. Unknowingly, they shape flexibility long before future capacity is clear.

Decisions that facilitate rapid progress early can quietly restrict future choices.

This book exists to slow that moment down.

The Smart Start RN focuses on early decisions because they carry the longest consequences—not because they are dramatic, but because they compound quietly. The goal is not to maximize income. It is to preserve space.

Introduction

This book was written to prevent mistakes, not to inspire urgency.

Most nurses do not need motivation early in their careers. What they need is orientation—clarity about which decisions matter, which ones do not, and which mistakes quietly cost decades.

At the beginning, most nurses do not feel financially reckless. They feel cautious, responsible, and focused on survival and competency. Long shifts, a steep learning curve, and emotional load make money feel secondary. As long as bills are paid and progress seems possible, details feel manageable.

That is exactly why this phase matters.

The earliest financial decisions rarely feel decisive. Debt feels temporary. Lifestyle upgrades feel earned. Scheduling feels flexible. Investing feels like something that can wait until confidence arrives.

But these decisions do not stay small. They define what becomes easy later—and what becomes difficult.

This book makes those early choices visible before they harden into obligations that future versions of you must carry.

The Problem Is Not Lack of Discipline

New nurses are often told they need better habits, more financial education, or stronger motivation. In reality, most are doing the best they can under pressure.

The issue is sequencing.

Advice built for stable schedules and predictable energy is often applied during a phase marked by night shifts, variable income, and exhaustion. Under those conditions, decisions tend to prioritize short-term relief over long-term flexibility.

That is not a personal failure. It is a structural one.

What This Book Is—and Is Not

This is not a guide to getting rich quickly.
It is not a budgeting boot camp.
It is not a test of discipline or ambition.

This book is about positioning.

Positioning means making smart decisions early so options remain open later. It means avoiding commitments that assume peak energy, constant overtime, or uninterrupted capacity. It means understanding how small decisions compound—not only financially, but structurally.

The goal is not to predict your future. It is to avoid foreclosing it.

At several points in the chapters that follow, you will encounter short worksheets. A few of these are drawn from the companion workbook and appear here in simplified form. They are not action plans or detailed programs. They are brief triage tools designed to assess load, exposure, and flexibility at moments where financial decisions tend to compound.

Their purpose is simple: to slow the moment down long enough to see what pressure is actually present. Each worksheet is optional, repeatable, and intentionally limited in scope. If one feels unnecessary, skip it. If one feels timely, that timing is information.

Some readers prefer to work through decisions on paper rather than mentally. For that reason, a companion volume—*The Smart Start RN Workbook*—contains expanded versions of these tools, along with decision-rule cards, scripts, and quarterly review pages designed to translate the framework in this book into practical actions.

Table of Contents

Quick Start: Find Your Starting Point in 5 Minutes

This book is built for real nursing conditions—fatigue, rotating schedules, and weeks that don't cooperate. Use this page to route yourself to the chapter that matches your constraint.

Step 1: Answer these three questions

1. **If you lost one shift of income, what would break first?**

   ☐ Rent/mortgage ☐ Car/transportation ☐ Food ☐ Minimum debt ☐ Childcare ☐ Other: ___________

2. **Is overtime functioning as a requirement?**

   ☐ Yes ☐ No ☐ Sometimes ☐ Unknown

3. **Do you have a buffer that can absorb a normal hit without panic?**

   (car repair, copay, urgent expense)

   ☐ Yes ☐ No ☐ Barely ☐ Unknown

Step 2: Go to the right chapter

If you need a foundation and want to avoid drift early
→ Chapter 1 – Start Quietly. Stay Free.

If monthly payments are shaping your choices (or overtime feels structural)
→ Chapter 2 – Debt Without Damage
→ then complete the **Financial Triage Worksheet**

If your baseline keeps rising under night shift conditions
→ Chapter 3 – Lifestyle Inflation and the Night Shift Trap
→ then complete the **Night Shift Financial Triage Worksheet**

If you keep delaying investing because you don't feel ready
→ Chapter 4 – Investing Before You Feel Ready
→ then complete the **Financial Triage Worksheet**

If you're deciding between jobs, units, or shift patterns
→ Chapter 5 – Choosing Jobs for Leverage, Not Just Pay

If you need perspective on the long arc (and what "wealth" really looks like)
→ Chapter 6 – The Millionaire Timeline (What Actually Happens)

If you want distilled hindsight and protective lessons
→ Chapter 7 – What Older Nurses Wish They Had Known

Step 3: Do one thing today (10 minutes)

Pick one:

- ☐ Put one bill on autopay

- • ☐ Automate one small transfer to your buffer

- • ☐ Capture your employer match (if available)

- • ☐ Write down your fixed obligations total for the month

- • ☐ Complete the worksheet tied to your chapter above

Status (circle one): Stable / Strained / Exposed
Next review date: _______________

A complete and detailed version available in the companion volume,
The Smart Start RN Workbook.

PART I:
STRUCTURAL FOUNDATIONS

(Capacity, Containment, and Leverage)

Before wealth compounds, structure must stabilize.

The first five chapters examine the mechanics that quietly determine whether financial progress requires constant intensity—or can occur under ordinary nursing conditions. These chapters are not about optimization. They are about durability.

Each section addresses a different structural pressure point.

1. Capacity

Nursing careers begin under strain. Irregular schedules, emotional load, and physical fatigue distort financial decision-making early. The first requirement of long-term freedom is preserving capacity.

Chapter 1 establishes the governing principle of this book: durability beats intensity. Financial decisions must function when energy fluctuates—not only when motivation is high.

2. Containment

Once capacity is acknowledged as finite, the next task is limiting structural risk.

Chapter 2 examines debt not as a moral issue, but as a behavioral force. When payments dictate staffing choices, flexibility narrows. Containment—not aggression—is the early objective.

Chapter 3 extends containment into lifestyle drift. Night shift pay and fatigue spending quietly harden into obligations. The goal is not deprivation. It is preventing temporary income from becoming permanent dependency.

3. Compounding Discipline

With obligations contained, consistency can begin.

Chapter 4 reframes investing as participation rather than mastery. Time rewards early exposure more than late precision. The task is not sophistication. It is sustainable contribution.

4. Leverage

Financial stability is not only about saving and investing. It is also shaped by work design.

Chapter 5 introduces leverage: job structure as a compounding variable. Pay is one dimension of compensation. Recovery, skill portability, benefits, and optionality often matter more over time.

Leverage determines whether income becomes freedom— or dependency.

Chapter 1:
Start Quietly. Stay Free.

Most nurses do not enter the profession thinking about wealth. They enter thinking about competence—about survival, about whether they can handle the pace, the responsibility, and the emotional weight. Money becomes something to address once things "settle down." That moment rarely arrives.

Early nursing careers are defined by instability: rotating schedules, night shifts, floating, inconsistent sleep, and constant learning. Financial decisions made during this period are rarely deliberate. They are reactive—shaped by exhaustion, urgency, and the understandable desire to make the strain feel worthwhile.

That is not a character flaw. It is a structural reality.

This chapter explains why starting quietly matters—and how it preserves freedom long after the early chaos fades.

The Early Career Illusion

Early income growth in nursing creates an illusion of momentum. Each raise feels meaningful. Overtime feels optional. Shift differentials feel strategic. It becomes easy to assume that if money tightens, the solution will remain simple: work more, pick up extra shifts, say yes a little longer.

This illusion is powerful because, early on, it is often true. But it is temporary.

What many nurses don't immediately see is that early decisions do more than shape cash flow. They build dependencies. They determine whether your life can function without overtime, whether your schedule remains flexible, and whether fatigue is an inconvenience—or a requirement.

The danger is not spending too much too early. The danger is building a life that only works under peak effort.

Freedom Is Built Before It's Needed

Freedom is rarely created at the moment it becomes urgent. It is built quietly, years earlier, through decisions that appear conservative, boring, or unnecessary at the time.

In financial terms, freedom means fixed costs that can be supported by base pay, debt that does not dictate your schedule, savings that reduce panic rather than merely increase balances, and investments that function without constant attention.

These conditions are easiest to establish early—before lifestyle expectations harden around higher income. Once obligations assume overtime, night shift, or relentless availability, freedom becomes expensive to reclaim.

Why "Quiet" Beats "Aggressive" Early On

Aggressive financial behavior is often celebrated in personal finance: maximum investing, optimization, side income, acceleration. For nurses early in their careers, this framing can be counterproductive.

At this stage, your most valuable asset is not money. It is adaptability. Your schedule will change. Your tolerance will change. Your understanding of what you want from the profession will evolve.

Quiet strategies preserve adaptability: modest fixed expenses, gradual investing, avoidance of irreversible commitments, and financial systems that function even when energy is low. Aggression narrows options. Quiet choices keep them open.

Money Decisions Are Energy Decisions

This is rarely discussed explicitly, but it matters for nurses.

Every financial decision carries an energy cost. Overtime requires recovery. Complex strategies require attention. High-maintenance lifestyles require constant income defense.

Early in your career, energy can feel abundant. That perception changes faster than most expect. Starting quietly acknowledges that future energy is uncertain—even if future income is not.

The goal is not to avoid effort. It is to avoid structures that require constant effort to survive.

The Compounding You Don't See Yet

Financial compounding is often framed as mathematics. But the most powerful compounding early in a nursing career is structural.

Small decisions compound into lower stress tolerance requirements, greater ability to say no, fewer forced tradeoffs between health and money, and more patience with investing and career moves.

These benefits do not appear on statements. They appear later—when others feel trapped and you feel flexible. That is the quiet payoff.

What Staying Free Actually Means

Staying free does not mean avoiding commitment or responsibility. It means not mistaking income spikes for permanent capacity, not normalizing exhaustion as a financial strategy, not confusing lifestyle growth with progress, and not assuming you will always want what you want now.

Freedom is not about keeping everything open indefinitely. It is about preserving enough optionality long enough for clarity to arrive.

A Different Kind of Advantage

Many early-career nurses assume they are already behind financially. That assumption is often built on the wrong comparison.

Nursing offers steady income, persistent demand, and a long earning runway. The structural advantage is not speed—it is durability. Nurses who avoid predictable early missteps often arrive decades later in a position few professionals reach: the capacity to slow down without destabilizing their lives.

That result is not brilliance. It is restraint applied consistently over time.

The Orientation This Book Offers

This book will not ask you to rush. It will ask you to notice which decisions quietly lock you in, which ones preserve optionality, which expenses assume peak capacity, and which strategies still function when you are tired.

Beginning with a measured approach is not passive. It is strategic. It preserves flexibility in the years that matter most. And flexibility, maintained long enough, allows time to do what urgency never can—compound.

Chapter 1 – Reflection Prompts

Designed to slow thinking—not accelerate action.

1. Which financial decisions I've made so far were shaped by urgency or exhaustion?

2. What assumptions am I currently making about my future energy or availability?

3. Which expenses or commitments would limit my ability to slow down later?

4. Where could restraint now preserve flexibility later?

5. What does "staying free" actually mean in my current life?

These questions are intended to encourage thoughtful reflection rather than prompt immediate answers.

They are designed to slow decision-making, allowing clarity to emerge before action is taken.

Minimum Viable Moves

For weeks when energy is limited.

- Write down your three non-negotiables: housing, transportation, and recovery. If those drift, everything drifts.

- Pick one "quiet" financial habit you can repeat weekly: a 10-minute review, a single auto-transfer, or a spending cap.

- Identify one place you are currently paying for speed (convenience, delivery, impulse fixes). Name it—don't judge it.

- Set one boundary that keeps the month from being rescued by overtime.

Where This Leaves You

This chapter does not ask you to act quickly.

It asks you to notice how early decisions shape freedom later—often before that freedom feels relevant.

If you leave this chapter more protective of your future capacity, more skeptical of urgency, and less tempted to prove progress through speed, it has done its job.

You do not need to win early.

You need to stay flexible long enough for time to work in your favor.

That begins by starting quietly.

What You'll Hear — and What This Book Says Instead

You will receive advice that sounds decisive.
Much of it is built for stable schedules, stable energy, and stable weeks. Nursing rarely provides that.

This book does not reject discipline.
It rejects plans that require constant intensity to remain functional.

Below are common messages—and the structural alternative.

"Just cut everything and grind it out."

What this assumes: surplus energy and predictable recovery.

What this book suggests: containment beats intensity.
If your plan collapses during a hard staffing month, it is not durable. Build a baseline that survives strain, not one that depends on momentum.

"Debt is always the enemy."

What this assumes: interest rate is the only relevant variable.

What this book suggests: the danger is debt that dictates behavior.
When payments make overtime feel mandatory, freedom narrows—even if the math appears manageable.

"If you're not investing aggressively, you're failing."

What this assumes: you can tolerate volatility and complexity without it affecting decisions.

What this book suggests: prevent obvious failure modes first. Capture matches. Automate consistency. Use durable defaults. Compounding rewards stability more than bravado.

"Take the higher pay. Always."

What this ignores: schedule instability, recovery costs, unit strain, and benefits.

What this book suggests: pay is a package.
A role that erodes recovery quietly increases spending and shortens longevity. The highest hourly rate is not always the highest lifetime outcome.

"If you really wanted it, you'd be better with money."

What this does: turns a systems problem into a character trial.

What this book suggests: exhaustion changes behavior. That is not moral weakness—it is institutional reality. The goal is not perfection. The goal is reducing how often your month requires rescue.

A final note: Your plan must function under nursing conditions. If it works only in an ideal week, it will fail in a real one.

Chapter 2:
Debt Without Damage

Debt is common in nursing because the sequence is backward: training precedes income stability, and life continues while schedules remain unpredictable.

The danger is not debt itself. The danger is debt that begins dictating staffing choices—overtime as baseline, differentials as requirement, job changes as unaffordable.

This chapter separates debt that preserves flexibility from debt that quietly narrows it.

The Problem Is Not Owing Money

Many nurses are taught—explicitly or implicitly—that the goal is to become debt-free as quickly as possible. That framing misses the real issue.

The problem is not owing money. The problem is debt that dictates behavior.

Debt becomes harmful when it requires overtime to remain current, assumes night shift or differential pay, reduces your ability to change roles, or narrows tolerance for rest and recovery. At that point, debt is no longer a financial tool. It becomes a schedule enforcer.

Scenario 2.1 – The Payment That Enforces Overtime

A nurse takes on a car payment that "fits" as long as she works two extra shifts per month. Initially, it feels manageable—until the unit grows heavier and she stops picking up shifts to protect her sleep. The payment does not shrink when capacity does. She bridges gaps with a credit card, then adds another monthly obligation to cover the first.

The issue is not the car. The issue is that her obligations assume staffing stability and energy she cannot control.

A protective default is to treat any payment that requires overtime as leveraged risk. Containment—reducing the fixed obligation through refinancing, downsizing, selling, or renegotiating—should occur before the obligation becomes structural.

Guardrails: When Debt Starts Enforcing Overtime

These are not moral thresholds. They are stress markers.

If non-mortgage monthly debt payments exceed roughly 10–15% of take-home pay, flexibility begins shrinking. Above 20%, "optional" overtime often becomes structural. If a single payment cannot be covered for one month using savings without panic, it functions as leverage regardless of interest rate. If a differential is required to meet minimums, the budget is staffing-dependent.

These are signals, not verdicts.

Why Nurses Experience Debt Differently

Debt advice is often written for stable, daytime, salaried professionals. Nursing operates differently.

Income may be strong, but schedules fluctuate, fatigue accumulates, recovery time is inconsistent, and emotional load is high. Debt that might be manageable in a lower-stress profession can become restrictive in one that already taxes the body and mind.

This is why identical debt loads can feel survivable for one person and suffocating for another. Context matters.

Training Debt vs. Lifestyle Debt

Not all debt deserves identical scrutiny.

Training debt includes student loans, licensure-related expenses, and required certifications. It is often unavoidable and can be justified by long-term earning capacity. The relevant question is not whether it exists, but how much control it exerts over early decisions.

Lifestyle debt includes cars sized to peak income, credit card balances used to relieve stress, and housing costs that assume overtime. It adapts quickly and locks in assumptions before sustainability is evaluated.

Training debt is visible. Lifestyle debt often hides in plain sight.

The Overtime Assumption Trap

Debt becomes damaging through assumption stacking. A raise leads to a larger car payment. A differential justifies higher rent. Overtime bridges the gap. Nothing appears reckless in isolation.

Over time, overtime stops being optional. It becomes structural.

When debt assumes extra shifts, your ability to recover, say no, change roles, or reduce exposure begins to shrink. Debt does not need to be large to do this. It only needs to be misaligned with base pay.

Debt as a Decision Accelerator

Debt accelerates decisions that should remain deliberate.

Under pressure, nurses may accept roles they would otherwise decline, remain in environments longer than intended, delay investing because cash feels tight, or avoid transitions that could improve long-term outcomes.

This shift rarely happens dramatically. It occurs incrementally until flexibility erodes.

Debt damage is rarely loud. It is cumulative and often invisible until later.

Containment Is Often Better Than Aggression

Early-career nurses are frequently advised to "attack" debt. That advice assumes stable energy, predictable schedules, and emotional bandwidth—assumptions that often fail under nursing conditions.

Containment—making debt predictable, manageable, and non-dominant—is frequently more effective than aggressive payoff strategies that collapse under fatigue.

Contained debt fits within base pay, has predictable payments, does not trigger monthly anxiety, and allows saving and investing to begin concurrently. Elimination can come later. Damage prevention comes first.

Debt and Identity

Debt also shapes identity.

Carrying high balances can quietly create a sense of being behind, pressure to "make it worth it," shame around rest, or a belief that strain must continue until elimination.

These interpretations are unnecessary. Debt is a financial condition, not a verdict. Worth is not measured by tolerance for exhaustion.

What Debt Without Damage Looks Like

Debt without damage does not require peak effort to manage. It leaves room for rest and flexibility. It coexists with saving and investing. It declines gradually without panic.

It may take longer to eliminate. But it preserves capacity while it exists.

That tradeoff is often rational.

The Quiet Goal

The goal is not perfection. It is to reach a point where debt no longer dictates schedule, forces decisions under exhaustion, or narrows the future unnecessarily.

When debt stops shaping behavior, it stops being harmful—even if it remains present.

That is success at this stage.

Chapter 2 – Reflection Prompts

Designed to slow thinking—not accelerate action.

You do not need to answer all of these. Choose one and respond briefly.

1. Where in my current financial life am I assuming peak energy as permanent?

2. Which expenses quietly require overtime or intensity to sustain?

3. If I reduced my effort by 20% next month, what would strain first?

4. What decision am I postponing because it feels "manageable for now"?

5. What would starting quietly look like in one specific area of my life?

If these questions create discomfort, pause there. That signal matters.

Minimum Viable Moves

For weeks when clarity is limited and energy is low.

Choose one. Not all.

• Calculate what your life costs on base pay alone.
• Identify one expense that assumes differential or overtime income.
• Set a 30-day pause on any new fixed obligations.
• Automate one small financial behavior that requires no weekly decision.
• Spend one pay cycle observing without changing anything.

The goal is not speed. It is alignment.

Structural Close

Freedom rarely appears dramatic at the beginning.
It is built quietly—through decisions that reduce dependency before dependency feels dangerous.

This chapter does not demand immediate elimination. It reframes debt as a structural force rather than a moral one. The goal is not perfection. The goal is containment—ensuring that obligations do not quietly dictate your schedule, your recovery, or your future options.

If you can see which commitments assume peak capacity, which payments require overtime to feel manageable, and which pressures narrow your flexibility, you are already ahead. Awareness comes before correction.

Debt becomes harmful when it shapes behavior.
Freedom expands when it stops doing so.

You do not need to win early.
You need to stay adaptable long enough for time to
work on your behalf.

That begins with restraint—and with structures that can
survive real nursing conditions, not ideal ones.

Using the Financial Triage Worksheet

Assess load, exposure, and flexibility before pressure
compounds.

This is not for solving everything.
It is for naming structure clearly.

Answer briefly. Skip what does not apply.

Financial Triage Worksheet

Date: _______________

Shift Pattern (days/nights/rotating): _______________
Current Role/Unit (optional):

____

Pay Period Type (weekly/biweekly): _______________

Average hours worked per week: _______________

Overtime required to feel financially stable?

☐ Yes ☐ No ☐ Sometimes

Current stress level related to money (0–10): _______

2. Financial Vitals (Quick Check)

Monthly fixed obligations (approx.): $_______________
(rent/mortgage, car, insurance, minimum debt payments)

Percentage of income already spoken for:

☐ <50% ☐ 50–70% ☐ 70%+

Emergency buffer (months of expenses saved):

☐ None ☐ <1 ☐ 1–3 ☐ 3–6 ☐ 6+

3. Exposure Assessment *(Where pressure accumulates)*

Check all that apply:

☐ My lifestyle assumes overtime rescue.
☐ My debt limits my ability to reduce hours.
☐ My financial plan depends on my body staying at peak
capacity.
☐ A schedule change would create immediate stress.
☐ I delay decisions because they feel overwhelming.

Primary source of exposure right now:

____

4. Flexibility Check _(What could change without collapse)_

If needed, could you within 60–90 days:

☐ Reduce hours without panic.

☐ Absorb an unexpected expense.

☐ Change shifts or units.

☐ Say no to overtime.

☐ Take unpaid time off.

Biggest constraint to flexibility:

____

5. Phase Recognition _(This is not failure—this is context)_

Right now, this phase feels most like:

☐ Early accumulation.

☐ Income growth with rising pressure.

☐ Capacity reduced / recover time long.

☐ Transition / uncertainty.

What has changed recently (energy, schedule, tolerance)?

____

6. One Calm Adjustment _(Not a plan. Not a fix.)_

If you were to reduce pressure slightly, what is **one** adjustment that would matter most?

☐ Lower one fixed obligation.

☐ Build a small cash buffer.

☐ Delay a lifestyle increase.

☐ Simplify, not optimize.

☐ Do nothing yet—just observe.

Status (circle one): Stable / Strained / Exposed

One action I will take before next review:

____

____

A complete and detailed version available in the companion volume, The Smart Start RN Workbook.

Chapter 3:
Lifestyle Inflation and the Night Shift Trap

If debt is the loud way obligations enforce your schedule, lifestyle inflation is the quiet way. Lifestyle inflation rarely arrives as excess. It arrives as relief.

When recovery is scarce, spending becomes a way to soften the edges of exhaustion. Over time, those choices harden into baseline expectations. The risk is not that life improves. The risk is what your obligations begin to assume about your energy, your schedule, and your continued access to differentials.

This chapter examines how income increases—especially night shift and differential pay—quietly become structural expectations, limiting freedom long before they feel dangerous.

Why Lifestyle Inflation Feels Deserved

Early nursing work is intense. You are asked to adapt quickly, carry responsibility early, and absorb stress that few professions normalize so casually. When pay increases, it feels earned—not indulgent. And often, it is.

The problem is not that lifestyle improves. The problem is what lifestyle begins to assume.

Spending decisions made during high stress tend to prioritize immediate relief over long-term flexibility. That relief feels reasonable in the moment—and quietly expensive later.

The Night Shift Multiplier

Night shift pay deserves particular attention because it alters perceived stability. Differentials and overtime create income that feels reliable, arrives quickly, and masks fatigue costs.

At first, nights feel strategic—a temporary acceleration phase. But when housing, car payments, and subscriptions are sized to include that extra income, the temporary becomes structural.

Night shift stops being a choice. It becomes a requirement.

That is the trap.

The Hidden Cost of Convenience Spending

Fatigue changes spending behavior. When cognitive load is high and recovery time is short, convenience becomes coping: food delivery replaces cooking, ride shares replace planning, online purchases replace pause.

These costs often appear small relative to income, yet they accumulate and reinforce dependence on higher pay.

A pattern emerges: work more to afford convenience, use convenience to survive work, normalize the cycle.

This is not primarily a budgeting issue. It is an energy management issue expressed in financial form.

Guardrails: Preserving Margin

You are not trying to track everything. You are trying to prevent drift.

If fixed obligations exceed roughly 55–65% of take-home pay, monthly flexibility narrows. If fatigue-related convenience spending routinely exceeds 5–10%, it often signals recovery scarcity rather than weak character. If a $300–$500 surprise requires overtime, the baseline is likely too high for current stability.

These are not rules. They are warning lights.

Lifestyle as a Schedule Enforcer

As lifestyle costs rise, they begin shaping behavior. They influence which shifts you accept, how long you remain in certain roles, whether you can step back during burnout, and how much risk you can tolerate.

At that point, lifestyle is no longer a reward. It becomes a constraint.

Constraints built early are harder to unwind later—
especially when energy is lower and responsibilities are higher.

Why This Happens Earlier Than Expected

Many nurses assume lifestyle inflation becomes a concern after
major promotions. In reality, it often occurs early because
income jumps quickly relative to baseline, financial literacy is
rarely taught alongside licensure, stress encourages immediate
relief, and peer norms normalize spending tied to exhaustion.

The danger is not extravagance. It is premature
permanence.

The Difference Between Enjoyment and Entitlement

Enjoyment is intentional and adjustable. Entitlement is assumed
and fixed.

Enjoyment can be reduced without panic. Entitlement
feels non-negotiable and triggers anxiety when income shifts.

The goal is not deprivation. It is keeping enjoyment
flexible.

A Better Use of Early Raises

Early raises and differentials are powerful not because they
enable more spending, but because they create margin.

Margin means faster recovery from difficult months,
less pressure to accept every shift, greater patience with
investing, and more freedom to change roles.

Using early income growth to build margin rather than lifestyle is one of the most underappreciated advantages nurses can create.

The Long View

Years from now, most nurses do not regret what they enjoyed early. They regret the structures they locked in without noticing.

A lifestyle that remains adjustable protects freedom. A lifestyle that hardens prematurely consumes it.

Chapter 3 – Reflection Prompts

Use these questions diagnostically, not judgmentally.

1. Which parts of my lifestyle currently assume night shift, overtime, or peak energy?

2. What expenses feel non-negotiable, and when did they become that way?

3. How much of my spending relieves fatigue rather than supports recovery?

4. If income dropped temporarily, which obligations would feel most constraining?

5. What would it look like to let future raises build margin instead of lifestyle?

You are not eliminating enjoyment. You are protecting flexibility.

Minimum Viable Moves

For weeks when energy is limited.

Choose one.

• Track only categories that can force overtime: housing, transportation, food, debt.
• Set one weekly cap for the fatigue-driven category most likely to drift.
• Automate one bill and one savings transfer.
• Choose one short review day each week. Consistency matters more than precision.

Progress is measured in preserved margin, not reduced pleasure.

Structural Close

Lifestyle inflation is rarely loud. It accumulates through reasonable decisions made under strain.

This chapter does not argue against enjoying your income. It asks you to distinguish between enjoyment that remains adjustable and structures that quietly harden into obligation.

If you can identify which expenses assume continued night work, overtime, or peak capacity, you have gained foresight.

Night shift can be a bridge. Bridges are not foundations.

Freedom is preserved when lifestyle remains flexible enough to survive a shift in energy, schedule, or priorities.

The goal is not to shrink your life. It is to prevent it from becoming structurally dependent on borrowed capacity.

In the next chapter, we turn to investing—where impatience can quietly undo the restraint you've just built.

Who Should Use the Night Shift Financial Triage?

Nurses working nights or rotating shifts, use this assessment to separate temporary compensation from structural assumptions.

Night Shift Financial Triage Worksheet

Date: _______________

Shift Pattern (days/nights/rotating): _______________
Current Role/Unit (optional):

____

Pay Period Type (weekly/biweekly): _______________

How long have you worked nights?

☐ <6 months ☐ 6–12 months ☐ 1–3 yrs. ☐ 3+ yrs.

Was night shift chosen primarily for:

☐ Income ☐ Availability ☐ Seniority ☐ Other: _______________

2. Income vs. Recovery Check *(What early income quietly assumes)*

Right now, does your financial plan assume:

☐ Continued night differential.

☐ Frequent overtime.

☐ Short recovery time.

☐ High tolerance for schedule disruption.

☐ "I'll fix this later" thinking.

Which assumption feels most fragile?

____

3. Financial Vitals (Night-Adjusted)

Monthly fixed obligations: $______________

Would obligations be manageable on day-shift pay alone?

☐ Yes ☐ No ☐ Unsure

Emergency buffer (months saved):

☐ None ☐ <1 ☐ 1–3 ☐ 3–6 ☐ 6+

4. Exposure Assessment *(What nights are holding up)*

Check all that apply:

☐ My lifestyle assumes night income.

☐ I delay saving because nights pay more.

☐ My plan depends on energy I'm already borrowing.

☐ I don't yet know my "baseline" without nights.

☐ I feel pressure to maximize income early.

Primary source of exposure right now:

____

____

5. Flexibility Check *(What could change without collapse)*

If nights ended in 60–90 days, could you:

☐ Cover core expenses.

☐ Reduce hours without panic.

☐ Absorb an unexpected cost.

☐ Adjust lifestyle downward.

☐ Say no to overtime.

Biggest constraint to flexibility:

____

____

6. One Early Adjustment *(Not optimization. Just orientation.)*

If you were to make **one** early decision that protects future flexibility, what would it be?

____

Status (circle one): Stable / Strained / Exposed

One action I will take before next review:

____

____

A complete and detailed version available in the companion volume,
The Smart Start RN Workbook.

Chapter 4:
Investing Before You Feel Ready

Most nurses delay investing for a simple reason: they don't feel ready.

Income still feels unstable. Schedules remain inconsistent. Debt exists. Life feels noisy. Investing gets framed as something you do after things settle down—after confidence increases, after knowledge improves, after money feels abundant.

That sequence rarely arrives.

This chapter explains why waiting to feel ready is a common investing mistake, and why starting early—quietly and imperfectly—matters more than precision.

Why Readiness Is a Misleading Signal

Readiness feels responsible. It suggests preparation, caution, maturity. In investing, readiness is often comfort wearing the language of responsibility—and comfort usually arrives too late to matter.

Early in a nursing career, income rises unevenly, knowledge feels incomplete, and financial confidence is low. Those are not signs you should wait. They are the conditions investing is designed for.

Investing does not reward certainty. It rewards time.

The Hidden Cost of Waiting

The cost of waiting is rarely dramatic. There is no single moment that announces the loss. The damage is cumulative.

When nurses delay investing, they often miss early compounding years, substitute saving for investing indefinitely, overestimate timing, and later feel pressure to "catch up" aggressively. That pressure increases risk-taking later—when energy is lower and mistakes are more expensive.

Starting early reduces pressure later. Waiting increases it.

Why "Understanding Everything" Is Overrated

Many nurses believe they should fully understand investing before participating. That belief is reinforced by complex language, fear of mistakes, and the idea that investing requires constant attention.

In reality, most successful long-term investors are not experts. They are consistent. They choose simple systems, automate contributions, and let time do the work.

Understanding improves gradually. Participation begins early. You do not need mastery to begin. You need exposure.

Simple Beats Sophisticated—Especially Early

Early investing should be boring. Broad-based index funds, retirement accounts, and automated contributions outperform complexity for most professionals—not because they are optimal in theory, but because they are sustainable in practice.

For nurses, sustainability matters more than strategy. A plan that requires monitoring, demands emotional regulation, or creates anxiety during downturns is likely to be abandoned. A simple plan that continues quietly—even when you ignore it—is more powerful than a sophisticated one that collapses under stress.

Safe Defaults (When You're Tired)

This book avoids precision pretending. The goal is not to beat the market. The goal is a durable baseline that functions even when schedules are unstable.

Account order (simple priority). If your employer offers a match, contribute enough to capture it. Treat that as baseline compensation, not a stretch goal. Next, choose one additional lane you can keep consistent. If high-interest debt is present, build a small buffer first so debt stops functioning as shock absorption.

Contribution default (sustainable, not heroic). Start with a percentage you can maintain through a hard month. Consistency is the point. Increase slowly when stability improves.

Investment default (boring on purpose). If you don't want to build a portfolio, don't. A single broadly diversified, low-fee fund—or a target-date fund—is a defensible default. Complexity is not a requirement for compounding.

A simple fee screen. If you don't understand what you're buying, treat that as a signal—not a challenge. High fees compound against you. Low-cost diversified defaults are usually safer than exciting stories.

What to avoid at the beginning. Stock picking as a learning plan. Frequent switching because the news feels urgent. Products you can't explain in one minute. Waiting to start until you "feel ready."

Your first job is not optimization. It is preventing obvious failure modes while you build time.

Investing as a Psychological Shift

Early investing does more than grow money. It changes how you relate to time.

When you invest early, income stops feeling like the only engine of progress. Pressure to extract everything from each paycheck decreases. Career decisions become easier to approach with patience. Urgency-driven strategies lose some of their appeal.

That psychological shift is often more valuable than early returns. It creates distance from panic.

The Myth of "I'll Start When I Make More"

Many nurses tell themselves they will invest once income increases. Higher income often arrives alongside higher fixed costs, greater responsibility, less flexibility, and more fatigue. When investing is postponed, lifestyle absorbs the raise instead.

Starting early—even with small amounts—creates a habit that scales naturally as income grows. Starting late requires willpower and restructuring. Habits formed under low pressure are easier to maintain than habits formed under urgency.

Investing Does Not Replace Stability—It Supports It

This book does not suggest investing instead of managing debt, expenses, or savings. It suggests investing alongside them.

Early investing is not about maximizing returns. It is about avoiding future desperation. When investing begins early, you are less tempted by risky shortcuts later, less pressured to "make up time," and better able to tolerate patience during career transitions.

Investing quietly now protects future choice.

What "Before You Feel Ready" Actually Means

It means starting while unsure, accepting imperfect knowledge, letting automation do the work, and allowing time—not intensity—to compound.

Readiness is not a prerequisite. Consistency is.

The Real Goal of Early Investing

The goal is not wealth yet. The goal is to reach a point later where money grows even when you rest, income pressure decreases, career decisions feel less fragile, and urgency no longer dictates your options.

That outcome depends far more on when you start than on how clever you are.

Chapter 4 – Reflection Prompts

Designed to slow thinking—not accelerate action.

1. What has made me feel "not ready" to invest so far?

2. Am I confusing comfort with preparedness?

3. What simple approach could I sustain during a hard month?

4. How might starting small now reduce pressure later?

5. Which fears about investing are really fears about making mistakes—and are those fears proportional?

Minimum Viable Moves

For weeks when energy is limited.

Choose one.

• If there's an employer match, contribute enough to capture it. That is baseline.
• Automate a small recurring contribution to one retirement account.

• Use a simple default investment (broad diversification, low fees).

• If you can't explain a product quickly, treat that as a signal—not a challenge.

Structural Close

Most nurses do not delay investing because they are irresponsible. They delay because they are waiting for calm—more knowledge, more confidence, more stability.

The problem is that calm rarely arrives on schedule. Investing is not reserved for perfect conditions. It is built for imperfect ones.

If you begin while uncertain but consistent, you reduce the pressure to "catch up" later. You also reduce the temptation to take risks under exhaustion.

Your first goal is not precision. It is participation that can survive nursing conditions.

Time compounds quietly. So do habits. Starting early—without drama—lets both work for you.

Financial Triage Review

Before increasing contributions, changing strategies, or taking on more risk, some readers may benefit from a brief structural check using the Financial Triage Worksheet introduced earlier.

The purpose is not to start over. It is to confirm that your investing plan rests on stable ground. If overtime is still functioning as rescue, if fixed obligations are stretched, or if recovery is already strained, increasing investment intensity may compound pressure rather than progress.

Revisit the worksheet with one question in mind:

Is my current structure durable enough to support consistent investing without requiring peak capacity?

Financial Triage Worksheet

(Reprinted for convenience)

Date: _______________

Shift Pattern (days/nights/rotating): _______________
Current Role/Unit (optional):

____

Pay Period Type (weekly/biweekly): _______________

Average hours worked per week: _______________

Overtime required to feel financially stable?

☐ Yes ☐ No ☐ Sometimes

Current stress level related to money (0–10): _______

2. Financial Vitals (Quick Check)

Monthly fixed obligations (approx.): $_____________
(rent/mortgage, car, insurance, minimum debt payments)

Percentage of income already spoken for:

☐ <50% ☐ 50–70% ☐ 70%+

Emergency buffer (months of expenses saved):

☐ None ☐ <1 ☐ 1–3 ☐ 3–6 ☐ 6+

3. Exposure Assessment *(Where pressure accumulates)*

Check all that apply:

☐ My lifestyle assumes overtime rescue.

☐ My debt limits my ability to reduce hours.

☐ My financial plan depends on my body staying at peak
capacity.

□ A schedule change would create immediate stress.

□ I delay decisions because they feel overwhelming.

Primary source of exposure right now:

---

4. Flexibility Check *(What could change without collapse)*

If needed, could you within 60–90 days:

□ Reduce hours without panic.

□ Absorb an unexpected expense.

□ Change shifts or units.

□ Say no to overtime.

□ Take unpaid time off.

Biggest constraint to flexibility:

---

5. Phase Recognition *(This is not failure—this is context)*

Right now, this phase feels most like:

□ Early accumulation.

□ Income growth with rising pressure.

□ Capacity reduced / recover time long.

□ Transition / uncertainty.

What has changed recently (energy, schedule, tolerance)?

---

6. One Calm Adjustment *(Not a plan. Not a fix.)*

If you were to reduce pressure slightly, what is **one** adjustment that would matter most?

☐ Lower one fixed obligation.

☐ Build a small cash buffer.

☐ Delay a lifestyle increase.

☐ Simplify, not optimize.

☐ Do nothing yet—just observe.

Status (circle one): Stable / Strained / Exposed
One action I will take before next review:

____

____

A complete and detailed version available in the companion volume,
The Smart Start RN Workbook.

Consistent investing is easier when your work structure supports recovery—and harder when your job demands constant intensity. When investing becomes consistent, the next leverage point is the job itself—because income and recovery determine whether consistency survives.

Chapter 5:
Choosing Jobs for Leverage, Not Just Pay

Once the basics are stable, job design becomes the next major lever—because pay is a package, and recovery is part of compensation.

Early in a nursing career, job offers are often evaluated using a single metric: pay.

Hourly rate. Differentials. Overtime potential. Sign-on bonuses.

This focus is understandable. Income matters—especially when debt exists and stability feels fragile. But pay is only one dimension of compensation, and often the most misleading one when viewed in isolation.

This chapter is about evaluating nursing jobs not only by what they pay today, but by what they make possible over time.

That difference—between pay and leverage—is where long-term freedom is built.

Why Pay Dominates Early Decisions

Early-career nurses are rarely taught how to evaluate job structure. School focuses on clinical competence. Orientation focuses on survival. Financial education, when present, centers on budgeting and debt—not on how job design shapes long-term outcomes.

In that vacuum, pay becomes the simplest proxy for a good decision. Higher pay feels safer. It feels validating. It feels like progress.

But pay alone does not account for what a job extracts in return.

What Leverage Actually Means in Nursing

Leverage is the ability to receive long-term benefit from a unit of effort.

In nursing, leverage often appears as schedule predictability, skill portability, employer benefits, structured training pathways, reduced burnout exposure, and time for recovery and planning.

A high-leverage job allows one decision to pay off repeatedly. A low-leverage job requires full intensity every time.

High Pay, Low Leverage Roles

Some roles offer strong pay but low leverage. These environments often rely heavily on overtime, operate under chronic staffing strain, rotate schedules unpredictably, and provide limited internal mobility.

In these roles, income is tightly tied to endurance. Progress depends on tolerating sustained strain.

This does not make such roles inherently bad. Many nurses begin here.

The risk emerges when they become foundational rather than transitional.

Moderate Pay, High Leverage Roles

Other roles offer moderate pay but significantly higher leverage. These may include predictable schedules, strong retirement matches, clear internal pathways, transferable skill development, and lower emotional or physical strain per hour.

While they may appear less impressive early on, they often allow more consistent investing, clearer financial thinking, fuller recovery, and longer career sustainability.

Over time, leverage compounds in ways that raw pay does not.

The Schedule Is Part of Compensation

Schedule predictability functions as income.

It reduces convenience spending, cognitive fatigue, recovery time, and financial mistakes made under exhaustion.

A slightly lower-paying job that stabilizes sleep and planning can produce stronger long-term financial outcomes than a higher-paying job that destabilizes everything else.

The effect is indirect—but powerful.

Benefits: The Invisible Paycheck

Benefits feel abstract early because they do not appear in a checking account immediately.

Retirement matches, pensions, healthcare coverage, tuition support, and paid time off are forms of delayed compensation—often at favorable terms.

A strong employer match can equal several dollars per hour in effective pay. A pension can reduce long-term pressure significantly.

Ignoring benefits because they feel distant is a common early-career oversight.

Skill Leverage and Optionality

Some roles build skills that remain valuable even as physical capacity changes. Teaching, informatics, case management, leadership, and outpatient roles often create transition pathways that preserve income with less strain.

Choosing roles that build transferable skills increases optionality later—even if early pay is lower.

Optionality is one of the most underestimated forms of wealth.

Why This Matters More Than It Appears

Early job choices set expectations about acceptable stress, normal hours, and how much of yourself is consumed.

Those expectations become habits.

Habits become norms.

Norms become difficult to unwind.

Choosing leverage early normalizes sustainability rather than extraction.

How to Evaluate Jobs Differently

- When comparing roles, ask:
- Does this job assume peak energy?
- Can I sustain this schedule for years?
- What happens if I need to step back temporarily?
- What skills will this role leave me with?
- How much of my future flexibility does this job preserve?

These questions often matter more than the hourly rate.

Job Leverage Scorecard (Pay Is a Package)

Use this to evaluate a job as a system, not a headline.

Score each item **1 to 5**.

1 = fragile / staffing-dependent

3 = workable but exposed

5 = stable / recovery-friendly

1. **Schedule Predictability**

   How often does your life get rearranged by last-minute changes, mandatory overtime, or inconsistent rotations?

2. **Unit Strain and Staffing Reality**

   Is the unit routinely short, high turnover, high acuity without support, or dependent on constant crisis staffing?

3. **Recovery Friendliness**

   Does the job leave you enough sleep and recovery to function without buying relief (convenience spending, constant takeout, impulse coping)?

4. **Benefit Package (Not Just the Match)**

   Health costs, PTO, sick time, retirement match, disability coverage—how much stability does the package buy?

5. **Skill Portability and Growth Path**

    Does this role build skills that travel across facilities and markets, or does it trap you in a narrow niche?

6. **Internal Mobility and Support**

    Are there real paths to transfer units, change shifts, or advance—without politics being the only gate?

7. **Commute and Friction Costs**

    Time, gas, tolls, parking, childcare logistics. Friction is an expense and a fatigue tax.

8. **Pay Structure Quality**

    How much of the pay depends on differentials, bonuses, or conditions you can't reliably control?

Total Score (out of 40): _________

Interpretation (guardrail, not law):

- **32–40:** High leverage. Job tends to preserve capacity and options.

- **24–31:** Mixed. Watch the weak categories—those become your hidden costs.

- **16–23:** Staffing-dependent. Overtime rescue risk rises.

- **8–15:** Fragile. High risk of burnout spending, instability, and forced trade-offs.

True Pay (Quick Estimate)

Headline pay is incomplete. Estimate the package:

- Add the annual value of **the retirement match** (if any).

- Add the annual value of **PTO you actually can use**.

- Subtract annual **out-of-pocket health costs** you expect.

- Subtract **commute and friction costs** (time + money).

If two jobs are close in hourly rate, the one with higher leverage often wins long-term because it preserves your ability to stay in the workforce.

Chapter 5 – Reflection Prompts

Designed to slow thinking—not accelerate action.

1. Which past job choices prioritized pay over leverage?

2. How has my schedule influenced my spending, saving, or investing behavior?

3. What benefits or skill-building opportunities have I undervalued?

4. If I were planning for my future energy, which job traits would matter most?

5. What would a "high-leverage" role look like for me right now?

Minimum Viable Moves

For weeks when energy is limited.

Choose one.

• Estimate your "true pay," not just hourly rate.
• Identify one leverage-building move for the next 90 days.
• Review your Job Leverage Score and circle the weakest category.
• If overtime makes a role feel worthwhile, treat that as a risk marker.

Structural Close

Most nurses do not feel trapped because of a single poor decision. They feel trapped because of a series of reasonable choices that prioritized pay without accounting for leverage.

This chapter does not ask you to sacrifice income. It asks you to evaluate what income costs in energy, recovery, and future flexibility.

Leverage often looks unremarkable early. It does not impress on paper. But it is what allows stability to persist when capacity changes.

A job that preserves your ability to rest, adapt, and build transferable skills compounds quietly over time.

Pay matters. But leverage determines whether pay becomes freedom—or dependence.

Quarterly Financial Review

Rather than treating this as a dashboard to maintain weekly, use it quarterly to assess structural stability.

Review:

• Buffer adequacy
• Fixed exposure and overtime reliance
• Fatigue spending drift
• Investing consistency
• Current Job Leverage Score

The purpose is not optimization. It is orientation.

If your structure is strengthening, continue. If strain is increasing, adjust early.

Financial Vitals Dashboard (Quarterly Review)

Date: ______________

Shift Pattern: ☐ Days ☐ Nights ☐ Rotating
Role/Unit (optional):

____

1) Buffer (Shock Absorption)

Current buffer amount: $______________

Covers essentials for: ☐ < 2 weeks ☐ 2–4 weeks ☐ 1 month
☐ 3+ months

Last time you used the buffer: ______________

Reason: ________________________

2) Fixed Exposure (Obligations That Enforce Behavior)

Total fixed monthly obligations: $______________
(housing + transportation + minimum debt + insurance +
required bills)

**Does overtime function as a requirement to cover fixed
obligations?**

☐ Yes ☐ No ☐ Sometimes ☐ Unknown

One obligation I will reduce/renegotiate next:

____

3) Drift (Baseline Creep Under Fatigue)

Top two fatigue-spend categories this quarter:

1. ______________________ Approx.
$__________/month

2. ___________________________ Approx.
$__________/month

What condition triggers it most?

☐ Short staffing ☐ Poor sleep ☐ Schedule changes ☐ Stress ☐
Other: __________

One containment rule I will implement:

4) Investing (Consistency, Not Complexity)

Employer match captured? ☐ Yes ☐ No ☐ Not offered ☐
Unknown

Automated contribution active? ☐ Yes ☐ No

Current contribution rate (if known): _________%

Default investment choice:

☐ Target-date ☐ Broad index ☐ Other: ____________

Do I understand what I'm invested in (1-minute explanation)? ☐ Yes ☐ No

5) Work Leverage (Capacity Preservation)

Job Leverage Score (out of 40): _________
Weakest category (1–2 items):

____

One leverage move for the next 90 days:

____

Status and Next Review

Status (circle one): Stable / Strained / Exposed

*A complete and detailed version available in the companion volume,
The Smart Start RN Workbook.*

Part I: Close

The first half of this book has focused on structural discipline.

Capacity preserved.
Obligations contained.
Consistency established.
Leverage considered.

Without these elements, financial progress depends on intensity. With them, progress can occur without constant strain.

What follows shifts from structure to trajectory.

Because once durability is in place, time becomes the primary force—and time, handled patiently, compounds more reliably than effort alone.

PART II:
THE COMPOUNDING TIMELINE

Capacity preserved.
Obligations contained.
Consistency established
Leverage considered.

The first half of this book focused on structure—ensuring that your financial life can function under real nursing conditions. Stability comes first. Without it, progress requires constant intensity.

Part II shifts from structure to trajectory.

Here we examine what actually happens over time when nurses combine steady income, controlled fixed costs, consistent investing, and leverage-oriented job decisions. Not in theory. In realistic progression.

We move from avoiding failure modes to observing compounding.

Because once structure is durable, time becomes the primary variable.

And time, handled patiently, changes outcomes more than precision ever will.

Chapter 6:
The Millionaire Timeline (What Actually Happens)

Most nurses carry a quiet expectation about money.

Not a precise number.

A timeline.

By a certain age, things should feel easier. Savings should feel visible. Progress should feel tangible. The future should feel more secure than it did at the beginning.

When that doesn't happen quickly, frustration sets in.

This chapter explains why that feeling is common—and why it is often misleading.

The Myth of Early Visibility

Wealth is largely invisible at first.

Early investing does not feel rewarding. Account balances grow slowly. Contributions appear small relative to effort. Market fluctuations create doubt rather than confidence.

This creates a false impression: that nothing is happening.

In reality, the early years are doing the most important work. They are laying the foundation for later acceleration. Foundations, however, are not impressive to observe.

Why the First Decade Feels Uneventful

In the first decade of a nursing career, most financial progress is absorbed by stabilization. Income increases replace instability rather than create surplus. Savings absorb emergencies. Investing begins but does not yet dominate outcomes.

This phase feels slow because contributions are modest, time has not yet compounded them, lifestyle adjustments are still occurring, and confidence is still forming.

Slow does not mean ineffective. It often means foundational.

Compounding Is Back-Loaded

Compounding does not reward early participation with early results. It rewards early participation with later acceleration.

Most long-term wealth growth occurs in the second half of the investing timeline—not because investors become suddenly brilliant, but because time begins to assert itself.

The early years require patience.
The later years reward it.

Why Nurses Feel "Behind" Even When They Aren't

Nurses often compare themselves to narratives that do not match their circumstances. Stories of early investors, rapid growth, and dramatic milestones dominate financial conversation. These stories are loud—but not representative.

Nursing careers often begin later due to training, include periods of reduced capacity, require physical and emotional labor, and prioritize stability over speculation.

Different paths require different timelines. Comparison without context creates unnecessary discouragement.

The Role of Income Growth

Income growth matters—but not in the way it is commonly framed.

Early income growth improves stability, reduces stress, and enables consistency. Later income growth increases contributions and accelerates compounding.

The key insight is this: early income growth supports investing. It does not replace time.

Trying to compress the timeline through income alone often produces overwork rather than durable progress.

The Emotional Lag of Wealth

One of the least discussed aspects of building wealth is emotional lag.

Even when progress is real, it may not feel real. Accounts fluctuate. Headlines amplify fear. Daily life remains mostly unchanged. This disconnect leads many professionals to abandon steady strategies in favor of something that feels more productive.

Consistency feels boring before it feels effective.

The Inflection Point

For many professionals, there is a gradual inflection point— often years after beginning—when the experience changes.

Not sudden wealth.
But reduced urgency.

Savings cover more than emergencies. Investments move meaningfully without increased effort. Career decisions feel less fragile.

This is not luck. It is accumulated time.

Those who remain consistent reach it quietly. Those who chase acceleration often interrupt the process.

Why Rushing the Timeline Backfires

Attempts to accelerate the timeline frequently involve overconcentration, excessive risk, complexity, or emotionally reactive decisions.

These approaches increase volatility and reduce sustainability—especially in demanding professions.

The timeline cannot be forced. It can only be respected.

The Milestone That Actually Matters

Net worth milestones are visible but incomplete.

A more meaningful milestone is structural independence from urgency:

When overtime is no longer required to absorb surprises.
When investing continues during busy periods.
When career decisions are not driven by financial fragility.
When patience replaces pressure.

That moment does not arrive dramatically. It emerges gradually.

A More Accurate Question

Instead of asking, "How fast can I get there?" ask:

Am I still consistent?
Is my structure intact?
Am I avoiding decisions that will create urgency later?

If the answers are yes, you are likely on track—even if progress feels quiet.

Chapter 6 – Reflection Prompts

Designed to slow thinking—not accelerate action.

1. What assumptions do I hold about how quickly wealth should appear?

2. Where has impatience influenced my financial decisions?

3. What evidence do I have that steady progress is working—even if slowly?

4. How would my behavior change if I trusted time more than urgency?

5. What would durability look like for me over the next five years?

Minimum Viable Moves

For weeks when clarity is limited.

Choose one.

• Review your investment contributions and confirm they are automated.
• Increase your contribution by a small, sustainable percentage.
• Revisit your buffer target and ensure it reduces reliance on overtime.
• Do nothing new—just confirm consistency.

Progress in this phase is measured by continuation, not acceleration.

Structural Close

The millionaire timeline is not dramatic. It is uneven at first and accelerating later.

Most frustration comes from expecting visibility too early. Wealth often compounds quietly long before it feels meaningful.

This chapter does not promise speed. It clarifies sequence.

If your structure is stable, your contributions are consistent, and urgency is decreasing, you are likely closer to the inflection point than you realize.

You do not need to compress the timeline.

You need to remain intact long enough for time to work.

Chapter 7:
What Older Nurses Wish They Had Known

This chapter is not about regret.

Most older nurses do not wish they had chosen a different profession. They do not wish they had worked less hard, or cared less. What they often wish is that they had understood how quietly the future arrives—and how early decisions shape it long before it feels relevant.

The lessons here are not dramatic. That is what makes them reliable.

Time Feels Abundant—Until It Doesn't

Early in a career, time feels generous. There is always another year to adjust, another contract to try, another stretch of overtime to recover from later. Financial decisions feel reversible because the future feels distant.

What older nurses describe is not that time disappeared, but that it stopped feeling expandable. Recovery took longer. Schedules felt heavier. Tolerance narrowed. Options that once felt open quietly closed.

The surprise was not aging. It was how quickly assumptions hardened.

"I Didn't Think It Would Add Up Like That"

Many older nurses describe the same realization: no single decision caused strain. No single expense felt excessive. No single year felt like a mistake.

But together, they accumulated.

A car payment chosen during night shift years. Housing sized for peak income. A habit of solving stress with spending. Investing postponed "until later." Nothing looked dangerous at the time.

The impact was cumulative.

Endurance Is Not a Financial Strategy

Nurses are trained to endure—to stay alert when tired, adapt when short-staffed, push through discomfort. These skills save lives.

But endurance does not translate well to money.

Older nurses often wish they had learned earlier that tolerating strain is not the same as building stability, sacrifice does not automatically compound, and being able to work more is not the same as being able to choose less.

Money rewards structure—not suffering.

"I Thought I'd Always Be Able to Do This"

This assumption appears often, not as arrogance but as normalcy. When capacity is high, it feels permanent. When health is good, it feels stable. When work is familiar, it feels manageable.

What changes is not willingness. It is capacity.

Older nurses often wish they had planned for the version of themselves that would want—or need—less exposure, fewer nights, or a slower pace. That version arrives whether planned for or not.

The Cost of Waiting to Invest

Many older nurses say the same thing about investing: "I thought I had time."

They were not wrong. They underestimated how long it takes compounding to feel meaningful.

Starting later did not make success impossible. It made it heavier. Contributions felt urgent rather than routine. Risk tolerance narrowed. Mistakes felt more consequential.

Starting earlier would not have changed effort. It would have changed pressure.

What They Were Glad They Did Right

This chapter is not only about missed opportunities. Many older nurses express relief about choices that preserved flexibility:

keeping fixed expenses modest, avoiding dependence on overtime, investing steadily even imperfectly, choosing roles with transferable skills, and protecting health before it demanded protection.

These choices did not make anyone wealthy overnight. They made later decisions calmer.

The Quiet Advantage of Restraint

Restraint rarely feels rewarding in the moment. It feels like passing something up, waiting unnecessarily, being cautious while others appear confident.

Over time, restraint compounds into fewer forced decisions, less panic during transitions, more options when energy declines, and greater dignity later.

Older nurses often say they wish they had trusted restraint sooner.

What This Chapter Is Really Offering

This chapter is not asking you to fear the future. It is asking you to treat it with respect.

You do not need to predict who you will become. You only need to avoid building a life that requires you to stay the same.

That is the lesson repeated most often.

A More Useful Question

Instead of asking, "Can I handle this now?" older nurses suggest asking: "Would I want this to still be true ten years from now?"

If the answer is no, the decision may still be acceptable—but it should remain temporary. Permanence deserves caution.

Carrying Wisdom Forward Without Regret

The nurses who speak most calmly about their careers are not those who avoided hardship. They are those who adjusted early, reduced assumptions gradually, let go of urgency, and built systems that supported change.

They did not escape work. They escaped panic.

Chapter 7 – Reflection Prompts

Designed to slow thinking—not accelerate action.

1. Which parts of this chapter felt familiar—or uncomfortable?

2. What assumptions am I making about my future energy or tolerance?

3. Which "temporary" decisions in my life are quietly becoming permanent?

4. What would kindness toward my future self look like right now?

5. If I could preserve only one form of flexibility, what would it be?

Minimum Viable Moves

For weeks when energy is limited.

Choose one.

• Identify one assumption your current life makes about your future capacity. Name it plainly.
• Reduce one fixed obligation or delay one new one that would be difficult to unwind later.
• Automate one small action that protects future stability (saving, investing, review).
• Make one decision temporary on purpose—with a clear review date.

Structural Close

Older nurses rarely wish they had cared less.
They wish they had identified earlier which assumptions were hardening into long-term obligations. The future does not arrive with an announcement. It arrives through accumulation—of habits, obligations, tolerance, and assumptions.

This book does not promise outcomes. It offers orientation.

If you finish more patient, more deliberate, and more protective of your future capacity, it has done its work.

You do not need to rush into the next phase. You only need to avoid closing doors before you know which ones you will want open.

Quiet starts become strong finishes when restraint is treated as strategy—not delay.

Epilogue – Staying Free Long Enough

This book was not written to make you fast.
It was written to make you durable.

Early in a career, speed is rewarded. Extra effort converts cleanly into extra income. Sacrifice feels temporary. Most decisions still feel reversible. That combination makes urgency tempting—and restraint feel unnecessary.

But time works best when it is not rushed.

The choices you make early do not need to be perfect. They need to be forgiving. They need to leave room for change, rest, mistakes, and growth that unfolds slower than expected.

That is what staying free means.

What You've Already Done

If you have finished this book, you have already done something important.

You questioned assumptions instead of absorbing them. You treated money as a system, not a test of discipline. You recognized that future capacity matters as much as present income.

Those shifts are quiet. They don't show up on pay stubs or resumes. But they compound.

You Are Allowed to Move Slowly

Nothing in this book requires immediate action.

If all you do is keep fixed expenses modest, avoid sizing your life to overtime, start investing without obsession, and choose jobs for leverage rather than exhaustion, you are doing enough.

Wealth that lasts does not require constant intensity. It requires time protected from unnecessary damage.

The Advantage You Can't See Yet

Early in your career, the advantage of restraint is mostly invisible.

You won't feel it until later—when you can say no without fear, change direction without panic, or slow down without everything breaking.

The future version of you will not remember the nights you could have worked.
They will remember the options you preserved.

Looking Ahead

This book stands on its own. You do not need to move on to the next phase until it applies.

But when income rises and effort stops converting the way it once did, you will recognize the shift. That is when the next conversation begins.

For now, your job is simpler: stay flexible, stay curious, stay free long enough for time to do its work.

That is how quiet starts become strong finishes.

Applying the Framework

Some readers prefer to work through decisions actively rather than just read about them. For that purpose, the companion volume **The Smart Start RN Workbook** provides practical tools that support the framework in this book.

The workbook includes:

• Financial triage and debt containment planners
• Night shift spending and recovery worksheets
• Investing default setup tools
• Job leverage and career decision scorecards
• Decision-rule cards to prevent costly mistakes
• Call scripts for negotiating rates, payments, and due dates
• Case-study decision pathways
• A quarterly financial review protocol

These tools are designed to help nurses move from understanding the framework to applying it during real working weeks.

Series Note

About the RN Wealth Series

The **RN Wealth Series** examines how income, work structure, and financial decisions compound across the full arc of a nursing career. Rather than focusing only on income, the series explores how scheduling demands, debt structure, recovery, and early financial choices quietly shape long-term financial stability.

Each volume focuses on a different stage of the nursing career, with companion workbooks that translate the frameworks into practical tools.

- **Book I — The Smart Start RN** focuses on early-career decisions that quietly shape future flexibility.

- Companion Volume: **The Smart Start RN Workbook** *Practical Tools for Money Decisions That Compound for Decades*

- **Book II — Stalled at Six Figures** addresses mid-career nurses who earn well but feel financially exposed.

- Companion Volume: **The Stalled at Six Figures Workbook**
  Implementation Tools for Turning Income Into Actual Wealth

- **Book III — Exit Vitals Stable** centers on stability, containment, and finishing a career intact as capacity shifts.

- Companion Volume: **The Exit Vitals Stable Workbook**
  Planning Tools for a Financial Path Out of Burnout

The books are designed to stand alone. They are not meant to be read in order unless that feels right. Some readers begin here and return to the others later. Others start elsewhere and come back when circumstances change.

There is no required path through this series. Each volume exists to meet a specific moment—so financial decisions can be made with context rather than pressure.

About the Author

Steve R. Reckons, RN

Steve R. Reckons is a registered nurse with a background in public administration and finance. He holds a **Master of Public Administration** and a **Bachelor of Science in Finance**, and has spent over **15 years** in the financial sector working in different capacities.

His work focuses on how financial decisions interact with professional capacity over time, particularly in nursing careers where schedules, energy, and tolerance for strain change across phases. Rather than emphasizing optimization or rapid wealth-building, his writing centers on structure, sequencing, and preserving long-term flexibility.

The RN Wealth Series reflects this approach— addressing financial pressure not as a personal failure, but as a predictable consequence of mismatched systems across different stages of a nursing career.

Where to Go Next in the RN Wealth Series

This book is the baseline. It is designed to reduce avoidable drift early—before income rises and obligations harden.

If you finish this book and recognize that your problem is no longer "getting started," do not force Book 1 to solve a later-phase constraint. Use the next book that matches your current condition.

If You Are Building the Foundation (Book 1)

Stay here if your focus is:

• preventing overtime from becoming a requirement
• containing fixed obligations
• building a buffer
• setting durable investing defaults
• choosing jobs for leverage, not just headline pay

Book 1 — The Smart Start RN
Money Decisions That Compound for Decades

Companion Volume
The Smart Start RN Workbook
Practical Tools for Money Decisions That Compound for Decades

If You Are Earning More but Feel Stuck (Book 2)

Move to **Stalled at Six Figures** if:

• your income increased, but your buffer did not
• you are "doing okay," but one disruption still forces overtime
• lifestyle baseline rose faster than flexibility
• you cannot tell where the money is going without a full audit
• you feel busy and paid, but not stable

Book 1 is about identifying where early financial decisions create pressure and how to build simple systems that allow money to compound rather than drift.

Book 2 — Stalled at Six Figures
How Nurses Turn Income Into Actual Wealth

Companion Volume
The Stalled at Six Figures Workbook
Implementation Tools for Turning Income Into Actual Wealth

Book 2 is about identifying where surplus is leaking, why it leaks, and how to convert income into retained flexibility—not just higher spending.

If Your Vitals Are Stable and You're Thinking Long-Term (Book 3)

Move to **Exit Vitals Stable** if:

• your buffer absorbs disruptions
• overtime is optional rather than structural
• debt no longer dictates job choices
• investing is consistent and boring
• you are ready to think in decades: mobility, exit timing, optionality

Book 3 — Exit Vitals Stable
A Financial Path Out of Burnout for Nurses

Companion Volume
The Exit Vitals Stable Workbook
Planning Tools for a Financial Path Out of Burnout

Book 3 focuses on keeping stability intact as responsibilities expand—so you can exit or downshift on your terms, not after burnout forces the decision.

The Point of the Sequence

Each phase has a different enemy:

- **Book 1 fights drift.**

- **Book 2 fights leakage and trapped surplus.**

- **Book 3 fights complacency and delayed exit planning.**

Each book can be read independently, but together they form a framework for navigating the financial realities of a nursing career over time.

About GAMS Relevance Press

GAMS Relevance Press publishes practical, systems-aware nonfiction for professionals navigating complex institutions, with a focus on work, money, health, and long-term stability— where decisions compound and structure shapes outcomes.

We prioritize clarity over hype and durability over trend, developing disciplined, practical frameworks built for real-world conditions and long-term relevance.

GAMS Relevance Press is an imprint of GAMS Relevance, LLC.

For new releases, publisher updates, media rights and inquiries:
GAMSRelevance.com
hello@GAMSRelevance.com